Glyph*

*a visual exploration of punctuation marks and other typographic symbols

Contents

Introduction

Glyphs are the building blocks of all written communication. They are the symbols that make up our language – the typographer's armoury and the type designer's work of art.

Some glyphs are loud and proudly announce their presence: 'Ay, Bee, Cee'.... Others are silent, yet no less important; they structure the pace of speech and order meaning into coherent sentences. Without them, words would be packed together in an indeterminate jumble.

These oft-neglected little things help us say more than words alone could do. Surprise! Bewilderment? Suspense... —silence.

This book is about all those quiet glyphs, the ones we tend to forget about. We want to celebrate their shapes and their history, and give these creatures their rightful credit after all.

Adriana Caneva, Shiro Nishimoto (Off-White) and Anna Davies

Comma — The word 'comma' comes directly from the Greek *komma*, meaning something cut off, or a short clause. It has its origins in the 3rd century, as one of a series of dots devised by Hellenistic scholar, Aristophanes of Byzantium, to indicate when to breathe when reading text out loud. Up until the 15th century, punctuation was generally used haphazardly with various marks, including the comma, colon and slash, used interchangeably to indicate how long one should pause for breath when reading a sentence. However, as society moved away from an oral culture to a written culture, the usage of punctuation became more regimented – serving a syntactic rather than an elocutionary role.

The modern comma still marks a pause in a sentence, but this is not a pause for breath, but rather in order to divide a sentence into smaller units, or clauses, so that it can be understood more quickly. Commas are also used to separate elements in a list, before quotations and to set off adverbs at the beginning of a sentence.

In typography, a well designed comma should encapsulate the essence of a typeface. As its shape is mirrored in apostrophes and quotation marks, these 'fringes' of punctuation act as visual anchors, enhancing and magnifying a font's language.

Full stop — The full stop is one of the easiest punctuation marks to master. It is placed at the end of a sentence to indicate that it is finished, and it has been used in its current form since the 9th century.

In the 19th century, the term 'period' was used to refer to a dot on the baseline that indicated an abbreviation, whilst a 'full stop' referred to the use of a dot to terminate a sentence. At some point in the 20th century, British English began to use 'full stop' as a generic term, whilst in American English the word 'period' was embraced. There are also divergences in the use of the mark between the Americans and the British. In American English, the full stop is used after all abbreviations. In British English, it is much more cautiously used, and is omitted if the abbreviation contains the first and last letters of the word (Dr, Mr) or in the case of acronyms (USA, UK).

In informal digital communication, the full stop is somewhat falling out of favour. The finality of a full stop can be construed as over-assertive or even aggressive. As a result, it is becoming more common to leave the end of a communiqué with no punctuation or with an ellipsis.

In typesetting, it was once traditional to use two spaces after a full stop, however since the advent of the computer, this practice is now obsolete, and a single space after a full stop is standard.

	1	2	3
a	●	◕	■
b	•	▮	▲
c	▮	⬬	◑
d	◎	▮	⬤

11

Colon — In the 15th century, the colon was one of the primary punctuation marks, indicating distinct clauses in a sentence, as a comma does today. When the comma made an appearance shortly after, the colon, semi-colon and comma were all used interchangeably – a practice that continued well into the 18th century.

The word 'colon' comes from the Latin *colon*, meaning a limb or a portion, and today it is generally used to connect the introduction of an idea and its completion. The clause that precedes the colon operates as a complete sentence, whilst the information that follows it proves, explains, defines or lists elements of the previous part, and may or may not read as a complete sentence. In this way it operates as a gateway – inviting the reader to carry on reading.

When typesetting a colon, it should sit on the baseline, just like any other punctuation. Spacing around a colon differs from language to language. In English, it is traditional to leave no space before a colon and a single space after it. In French and other European languages, however, it is common to place a thin space before a colon and a thick space after it. In American English, the first letter after a colon must be capitalised, but in British English this is not the case.

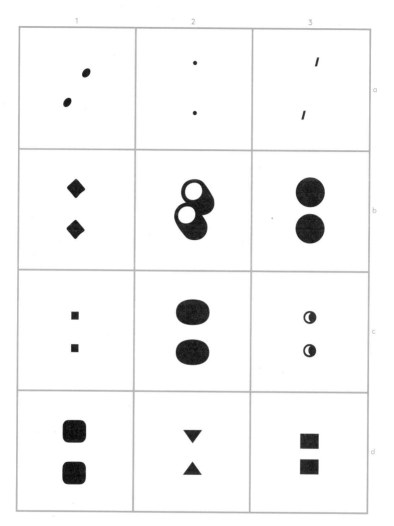

	1	2	3

1a Libelle Pro Regular
1b Goudy Old Style Regular
1c CaseStudyNo1 Light
1d OCR A Regular
2a SangBleu BP Hairline

2b Magnifico Daytime ITC
2c Antique Olive Std Nord
2d Kino MT Regular
3a Neue Haas Unica W1G
   UltraLight Italic

3b Cooper Black Roman
3c Imprint MT Shadow Reg
3d A. Ali Regular

Semi-colon — The semi-colon is one of the most disputed punctuation marks in the English language. George Orwell famously wrote an entire book without using a single one, and Kurt Vonnegut shrugged them off, stating, 'all they do is show you've been to college'. It is true that a semi-colon can often be replaced with a less ambiguous comma, conjunction or full stop, however the versatility of the semi-colon can offer stylistic freedom and provide a refreshing break in rhythm.

The primary use of a semi-colon is to connect two related but independently functioning clauses. It is often described as 'stronger than a comma, but weaker than a full stop'. Unlike the 'limb' colon, which works as an extension of the sentence's body, the semi-colon operates like handcuffs connecting two separate people. Semi-colons are also used between items in a series that already contains commas. A lower case letter should always follow a semi-colon.

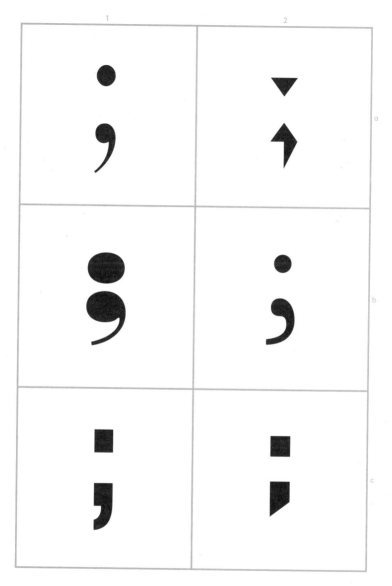

1a Modern20 BT Roman

1b Bodoni Std Poster

1c Helvetica Neue 77

2a Kino MT Regular

2b Plantin Infant MT Std Reg

2c DIN 1451 Mittelschrift

Apostrophe — The word 'apostrophe' comes from the classical Greek phrase, *prosoidia apostrophos*, meaning 'accent of turning away'. It was introduced in the 16th century to indicate a missing syllable or letter – such as 'don't' instead of 'do not'. In Old English (around 1100–1500), the possessive ending for nouns was 'es'. A book belonging to John, for example, would be 'Johnes book'. This was often misheard as 'his', and so, to avoid confusion, the 'e' began to be omitted, with an apostrophe taking the place of the missing letter.

Today, the apostrophe continues to mark the contraction of words and the possessive. In strictly limited cases, it is allowed to assist in marking the plural of a word that isn't recognised as an official word, (dot your I's and cross your T's), but even these uses are contentious.

Typographically, the apostrophe is often confused with the prime symbol ('), used for measurement in feet or inches, the acute symbol ('), which is used on top of letters as an accent, and the grave (`), also used for other accents in Latin alphabets. Apostrophes should always point down. If a word processor has flipped an apostrophe automatically, such as the first apostrophe in rock 'n' roll, make sure to flip it back around. Some argue that it should also always face left, towards the missing letter.

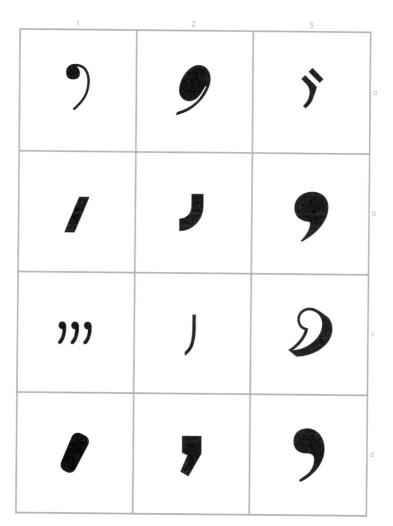

1a Bauer Bodoni Regular
1b A. Coupé Regular
1c Sobriquet Tripple
1d Mercury Bold

2a Stilla Regular
2b Arcus Regular
2c Neue Haas Grotesk Dspl 15
2d GT Cinetype Bold

3a Colonna MT Regular
3b Balega Regular
3c Gill Sans Shadow MT Reg
3d ITC Caslon 224 Std Black

( ) [ ] { }

Brackets — Always used in pairs, brackets serve to separate text from the context of a sentence. The word 'bracket' is derived from the French *braguette*, meaning codpiece, and the Latin *braca*, meaning breeches.

In typography, brackets should be centred vertically next to the text. This usually is part of a typeface's design, but in certain caps sentences or in the use of lining figures, you may need to slightly raise the brackets. Another issue to look out for is italic characters that occasionally collide with a bracket. In this instance, italicising the brackets affords a less jarring effect.

Parentheses are the most common type of bracket. The word comes from the Ancient Greek and literally means 'to put beside'. Parentheses behave like radical commas, setting apart information that is supplementary to a sentence. As well as enclosing explanatory, qualifying or incidental material, parentheses are also used to offset items such as abbreviations, area codes, numbered lists and acronyms. The surrounding sentence must make grammatical sense without the material inside the parentheses.

Square brackets or crotchets serve a similar purpose to parentheses, but are almost exclusively used inside quoted material, and are therefore far less common. Square brackets are also used to enclose material within parentheses, to avoid the use of parentheses within parentheses.

Curly brackets (also known as braces) only occur in specific circumstances in poetry, music, computer programming and mathematics, and should never be used to replace parentheses or square brackets.

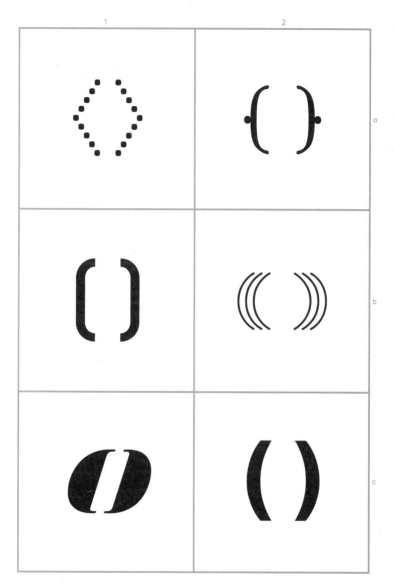

1a A. ABF Petit Regular
1b GT Walsheim Medium

1c Stilla Regular
2a Saphir Regular

2b Sobriquet Tripple
2c Neue Haas Grotesk Text 75

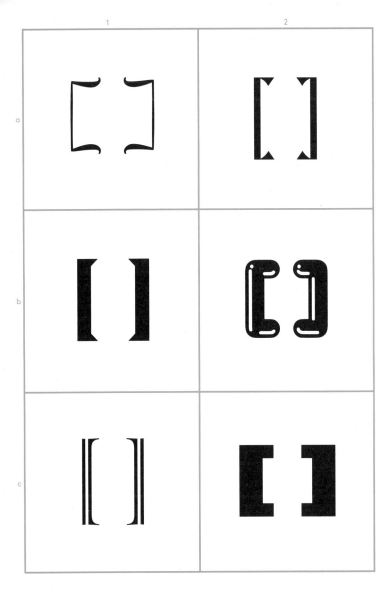

	1	2
a		
b		
c		

1a Bell MT Regular
1b Beirut Poster

1c Colonna MT Regular
2a Kino MT Regular

2b Frankfurter Highlight
2c Gill Sans Ultra Bold

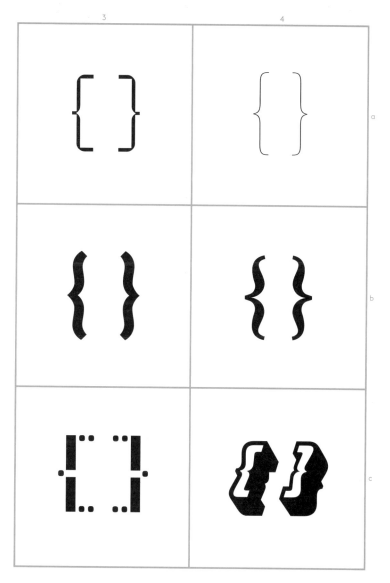

3a CaseStudyNo1 Pro Light   3c A. ABF Petit Regular   4b Larish Neue Semibold
3b Carrosserie Regular   4a NewParis KingSize Bold   4c Magnifico Daytime ITC

/

Slash — The word 'slash' first appeared in medieval times to mean a slicing movement by a knife or weapon (derived from the Old French *esclachier*). It's easy to see how this word was then transposed onto the dynamic diagonal slit that is the slash.

In medieval manuscripts, slashes were used rampantly in place of today's comma, but today the slash has limited uses. Its most common function is to substitute the word 'or' (Sir/ Madam, Y/N). It is also used to make a strong connect between words or phrases (love/hate), to replace per (km/h) and to indicate the end of a line in a poem or song. In recent years, the slash has become known as the forward slash, to differentiate it from the backslash, which is used only in computing.

Typographically speaking, it is worth noting the difference between the solidus and the slash (also known as virgule). The solidus is a mark used to denote fractions and is at a close to 45-degree angle. The slash is used in punctuation and is more vertical in orientation. However, today there is little differentiation between them and where there is no option of a solidus, a slash is generally acceptable. There are usually no spaces on either side of a slash, unless it's indicating the end of a line of verse.

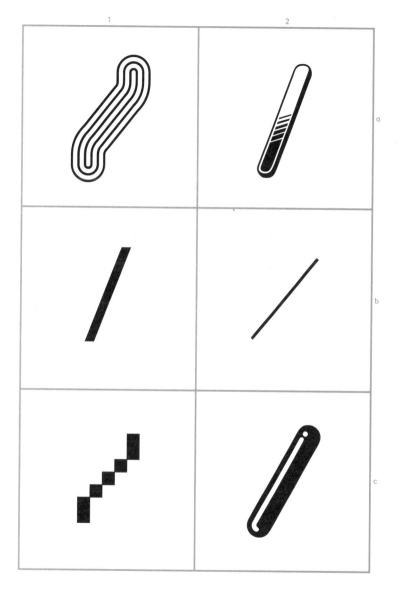

a

b

c

1a Stoneheure Regular   1c Screenex Regular   2b Libelle Pro Regular
1b Neue Haas Grotesk Text 55   2a Cabaret Regular   2c Frankfurter Highlight

The terms en dash and em dash date back to the days when type was set by hand on separate pieces of lead. The en dash was set on a piece the width of the letter 'n', and the em dash was a line the width of the letter 'm'. The hyphen is a character that was introduced much later with the advent of early typewriters. In order to keep the keyboard contained, the en dash, em dash and minus sign were compiled into a single 'hyphen' character.

Today, however, the hyphen is only used inside words to separate their parts from each other. The em dash and en dash have more complex uses. The en dash traditionally indicates an interval or range (10–12 or London–York). In American English, the em dash separates major parts of the sentence or sets off parenthetical elements where a semi-colon is too strong and a comma is too weak. However, in the UK and Canada, the en dash is often used in place of the wider, more obtrusive em dash to serve the 'setting apart' function.

If using an en dash to separate parts of a sentence, one should put a letter space on either side. The longer em dash traditionally has no space around it. This sometimes looks a little claustrophobic, however, and it is a matter of stylistic preference whether or not a thin space is inserted on either side.

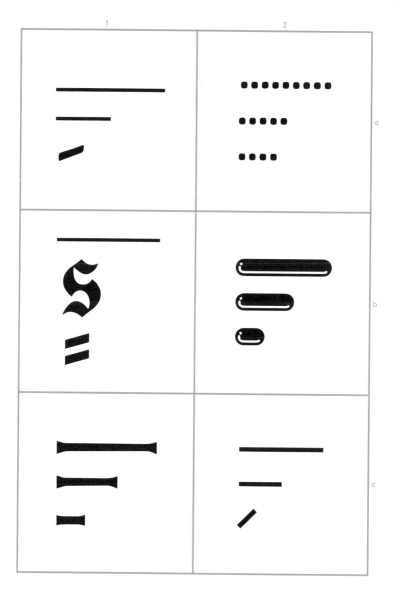

1a Goudy Old Style Regular
1b Wittenberger Fraktur Bold

1c Albertus MT Pro Light
2a A. ABF Petit Regular

2b Frankfurter Highlight
2c Custodia Pro Normal

" "

Quotation marks — The quotation mark has its roots in the diple symbol – which looked like an arrow (>) and was used to highlight important parts of a text and quotes from the Bible. In the 5th century, the monk, theologian and scholar, Rufinus of Aquileia, used a single diple to indicate his own arguments and a double diple to indicate the arguments of his opponents. The comma eventually superseded the diple, but a similar use of 'double commas' was used in the 16th century in the margins of lines containing quoted text. They gradually migrated into the body of the sentence to denote quotations and direct speech. Today, quotation marks are set around quoted or spoken material, unusual or slang words or around titles.

In American English, double quotation marks are primary quotations, and if there's a quote within a quote, a single quote is used. In British English, this is reversed – single quote marks are primary and double quotes are secondary.

Badly typeset quotes can be disruptive to the visual flow of the text and many designers prefer to use hanging quotation marks, which step outside the text box, allowing for a clean edge.

a

b

c

d

1a Johnston ITC Pro Light
1b Saphir Regular
1c A. ABF Petit Regular
1d Broadway Engraved BT

2a Goudy Old Style Regular
2b Univers 45 Light
2c Libelle Pro Regular
2d DIN 1451 GRK Mittelschrift

3a Times New Roman Bold
3b Gill Sans Ultra Bold
3c Algerian Regular
3d Wittenberger Fraktur Bold

!

Exclamation mark — The exclamation mark, known throughout the ages as admiration mark, screamer, shriekmark or bang, is used at the end of an exclamatory sentence to indicate strong feelings, emphasis or high volume. The mark is thought to have originated from the Latin word for joy, *io*, which was written vertically to resemble the exclamation mark we use today.

In serious prose and journalism, the exclamation mark has been much derided through the ages. F Scott Fitzgerald stated, 'an exclamation mark is like laughing at your own jokes'. Typewriters before the '70s did not even have a dedicated exclamation mark key – typists would have to write a full stop, then go back and add an apostrophe over it. However, in modern writing, the exclamation mark is making a comeback. As digital communication becomes the dominant form of interaction, it becomes ever more important to highlight the emotions behind written text. Where the exclamation mark was traditionally used to convey strong feeling – anger, surprise or joy – it has become a popular means of conveying lower key emotion, such as reassuring friendliness, enthusiasm or scepticism. Even multiple exclamation marks have become commonplace, merely adding conversational emphasis to a sentence.

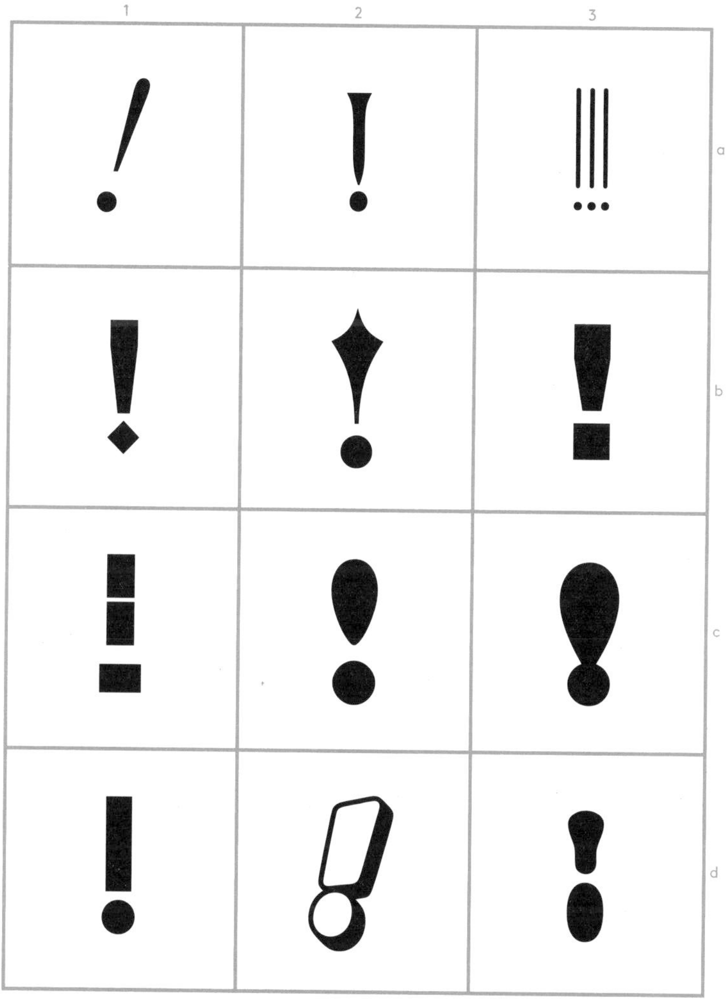

1a Baskerville MT Italic
1b Johnston ITC Pro Bold
1c Letterbox Pro
1d Futura CE Condensed Bold

2a Albertus MT Pro Light
2b Algerian Regular
2c Cooper Black Regular
2d Artiste Std Regular

3a Sobriquet Tripple
3b Neue Haas Grotesk Dspl 93
3c Gill Sans Ultra Bold
3d Bottleneck

?

Question mark — **Some believe that the question mark is derived from the Latin word, *questio*, which was placed at the end of an interrogative clause. The full word was abbreviated to 'qo', and eventually squashed into a symbol of a lowercase 'q' on top of an 'o', which in turn evolved into a dot and a squiggle – the question mark as we know it. Another theory is that the question mark descended from the semi-colon, which, at various points in history, was placed at the end of queries.**

In the 17th century there was much debate as to whether a question mark should follow indirect questions (such as, 'he asked me how I was feeling').

Further debate raged as to whether a *pointe d'ironie*, a reversed question mark, should be placed after rhetorical questions. The answer to both these debates was and is, no. The question mark is only used after direct questions, and rhetorical questions should end with a full stop.

In formal prose, the question mark should not be used in conjunction with other marks. However, in informal writing it is common to combine it with the exclamation mark to indicate incredulity.

1a Frankfurter Inline
1b Screenex Regular

1c Caslon 224 Std Black
2a Johnston Pro Medium

2b Gill Sans Extra Bold
2c A. Ali Regular

1a Bell MT Italic
1b Nord Black

1c NewParis KingSize Bold
2a Gill Sans Ultra Bold

2b A. ABF Petit Regular
2c Futura Medium

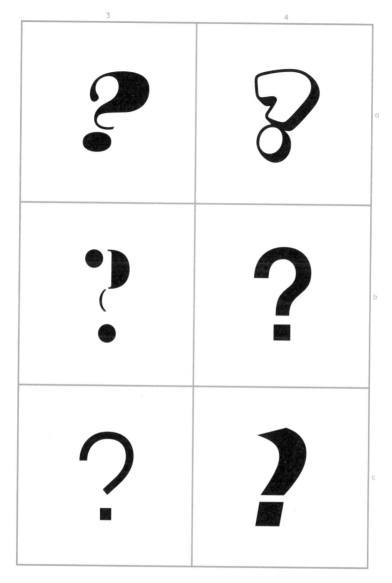

3a Stilla Regular
3b Iwan Stencil Pro

3c A. Coupé Regular
4a Artiste Std

4b Helvetica Neue 65
4c Banco Regular

Interrobang — The interrobang is a combination of an exclamation mark and a question mark. Advertising executive, Martin Speckter, introduced it in 1962, pitching it as a 'typographically eloquent way in which to end a statement that expresses excited disbelief, asks a question in an excited manner, or proposes a rhetorical question'. Speckter called his mark 'interrobang' from the Latin for query and the proofreader's term for exclamation, although the term 'quexclamation mark' is still used by some.

The interrobang was enthusiastically embraced for a brief period until the late '60s. An interrobang key was even introduced to some ranges of typewriters. However, the fad soon lost momentum, and the age old ?! combination was reinstated. Today it is still possible to find the interrobang in some fonts, such as Palatino, and it is recognized in informal English as a non-standard punctuation mark. It many ways one could say that the interrobang has now been superseded by the emoticon, which makes similar use of glyph combinations in order to add emphasis and feeling to the sentence that precedes it.

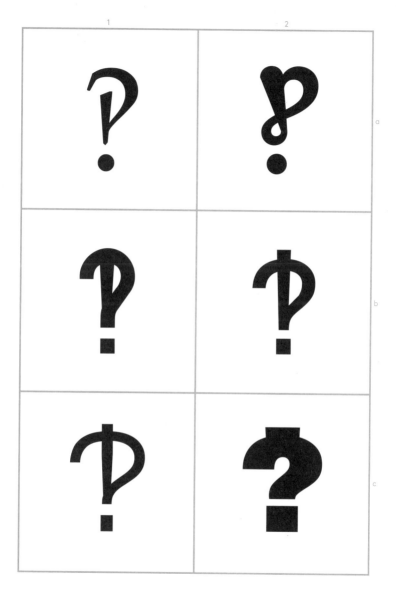

1a Palatino Linotype Regular   1c Helvetica Neue Light Ext.   2b Neue Haas Unica Regular
1b DIN 1451 Mittelschrift   2a Larish Neue Semibold   2c NeueHaasUnica ExtraBlack

"

Ditto — The ditto mark is a set of straight quotation marks indicating that a word or phrase given in the line above is to be repeated. The word is derived from the Latin word *dictus*, meaning 'having been said'. It was first used in the English language in 1625, but there is evidence of similar double line use indicating repetition as early as the 7th century.

When using a ditto mark, it should be placed directly underneath the word or phrase to be repeated. As a result, ditto marks are most often used in lists, to avoid writing again words that are immediately written above.

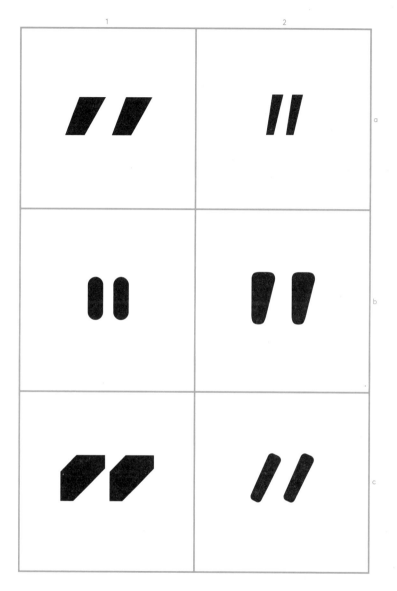

1 2

a
b
c

1a Univers 63
1b Singolo Regular

1c Letterbox Pro
2a Univers 39

2b OCR A Regular
2c Mercury Light

• • •

Ellipsis — Of Greek origin, ellipsis literally means 'to leave out'. It is a series of three dots that indicates an omission, a pause or an unfinished thought or statement. Aposiopesis is the use of an ellipsis to trail off into silence – literally a dot dot dot.

Typesetting ellipses is a tricky matter. Some say that the ellipsis should comprise three full stops with no spaces between them (...). Others specify a space between each dot (. . .) and still others prefer to use the single character glyph (…). In his book, *Elements of Typographic Style*, Robert Bringhurst dismisses the idea of a full space between each dot as a 'Victorian eccentricity'. If using the three-dot option, make sure that none of the dots go over the line break.

When the ellipsis indicates missing words it is usually set inside brackets or has a letter space either side. When used as a pause or unfinished thought, there is no letter space preceding it. At the end of the sentence, an ellipsis should be followed by a full stop (a total of four dots).

The ellipsis is experiencing something of a renaissance today. In the age of digital communication, we are ever more cautious not to be misunderstood in our tone and intentions. Where a full stop shuts down conversation, an ellipsis evokes uncertainty and vulnerability, indicating that we are open to persuasion....

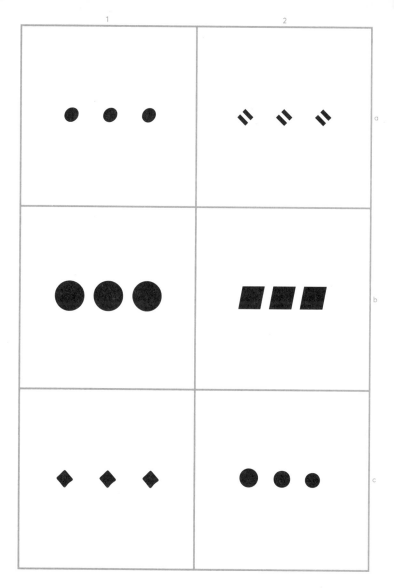

a

b

c

1a Avenir 55 Oblique
1b Gill Sans Ultra Bold

1c Goudy Old Style Bold
2a Colonna MT Regular

2b Neue Haas Grotesk Dspl 96
2c Larish Neue Semibold

&

Ampersand — The ampersand is a symbol representing the word 'and'. Its graphic form dates back to the 1st century, originating as a ligature of 'e' and 't' (et meaning 'and' in Latin). In certain typefaces the two letters are still discernible. The word 'ampersand' is more recent, originating in the early 19th century, when '&' was the 27th letter in the English alphabet, called 'and'. At that time, the words 'per se' preceded any letter of the alphabet that could be used as a word by itself (such as 'a' or 'I'), therefore, '&' was called 'per se and'. When the alphabet was recited, it would end, 'X, Y, Z and per se and'. Over the years this was slurred together into 'ampersand'.

Ampersands today are used in fairly specific circumstances. They should not be used within the structure of a sentence as a substitute for the word 'and', but are most commonly used in titles, business names and logos. There is an implied intimacy to the symbol, giving a sense of equal weight to the name or word that precedes the ampersand and the one that follows. In film credits, for example, 'writer's name & writer's name' indicates a collaborative writing process, whereas 'writer's name and writer's name' indicates two writers, who may have worked on the script at separate points, generally with the first named writer being of greater significance than the second.

The ampersand has one of the broadest variations of representation of any graphic symbol. Its calligraphic forms are often wildly elaborate, whilst sans serif typefaces are generally drawn with a single stroke in uniform width. A more casual, retro-style of ampersand can look like a backwards 3, with small strokes above and below.

a

b

c

1a Diotima Italic
1b Gill Sans Ultra Bold

1c Baskerville Pro Italic
2a Frankfurter Highlight

2b Magnifico Daytime ITC
2c Albertus Pro Light

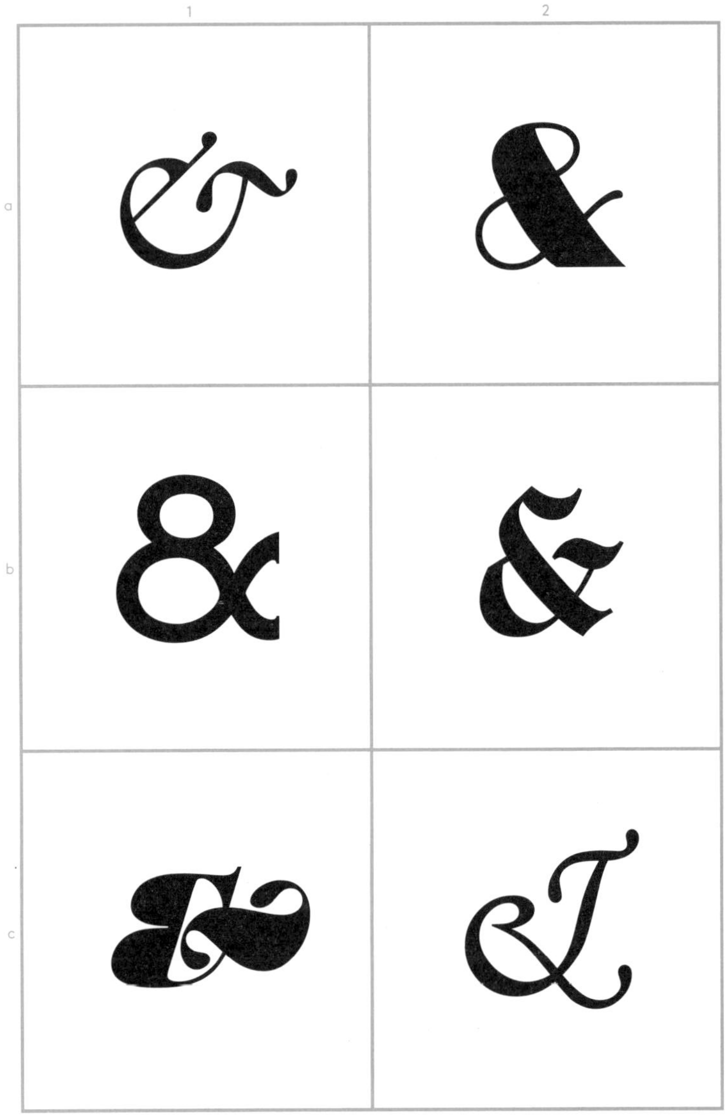

1a Galliard Pro Italic
1b Copperplate Gothic 32AB
1c Stilla Regular
2a Broadway Regular
2b Wittenberger Fraktur Bold
2c Monotype Corsiva Reg

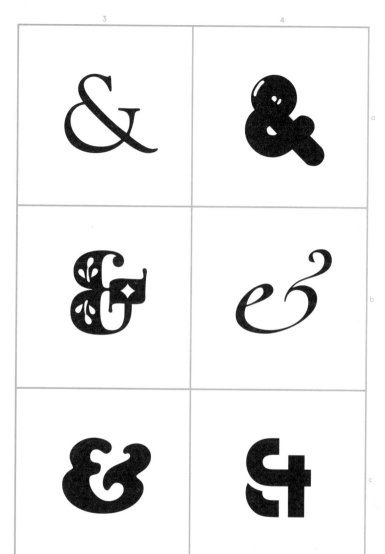

3a Goudy Old Style Regular   3c Cooper Black Roman   4b Cochin Pro Italic
3b Saphir Regular   4a Glowworm Regular   4c Glaser Stencil Regular

Asterisk — Derived from the Greek, *asteriskos*, meaning 'little star', the asterisk is exactly that. Dating back to Ancient Greece, the asterisk indicated that there was a query regarding the text, or that there was supplementary material. By the 18th century, numbers had replaced the asterisk as a more pragmatic form of footnoting material, however, the asterisk was still used in short texts and informal pieces of writing.

Today, the asterisk continues to be used for informal footnotes, as a way of adding information without the academic stuffiness of numbering. In this instance, the supplementary material generally features on the same page as the asterisk. In public records, an asterisk features next to the year of a person's birth. The symbol is also used to indicate censorship or the omission of an expletive (such as 'oh s***!'), as a typographical replacement to bullet points and in mathematics and computer programming. In recent years, the asterisk has become commonly used in social and textual media to represent emphasis or as a kind of stage direction (*sighs*, *coughs loudly*).

The original shape of an asterisk was seven armed, with each arm forming a raindrop shape pointing to the centre. Today, however, the asterisk can assume numerous forms and can have any number of arms; between five and eight is common, but they have been known to feature up to 12.

†‡

Dagger — The dagger (also known as the obelisk), evolved from the obelus symbol (see pp. 66–67). Since ancient times, the dagger has often gone hand in hand with the asterisk, but where the asterisk historically indicated the addition of supplementary matter, the dagger indicated the deletion of dubious material. This practice continued through medieval times, when it was also used to indicate a pause in the chanting of psalms.

Today, the dagger still complements the asterisk. Its most common use is as a footnote marker when an asterisk has already been used. It also features in public records – where an asterisk indicates the year of birth, the dagger represents the year of death. The dagger also represents death or obsolescence in a number of other fields: In biology, if a species is marked with a dagger, it means it is extinct. In chess, a dagger signifies that a move resulted in check, and in the *Oxford English Dictionary*, the dagger indicates that a word has become obsolete.

Typographic representations vary from a symbol that looks like a crucifix to a more stylized, Gothic-looking dagger. In some languages, such as German, daggers are used much less frequently due to their similarity to the Christian cross.

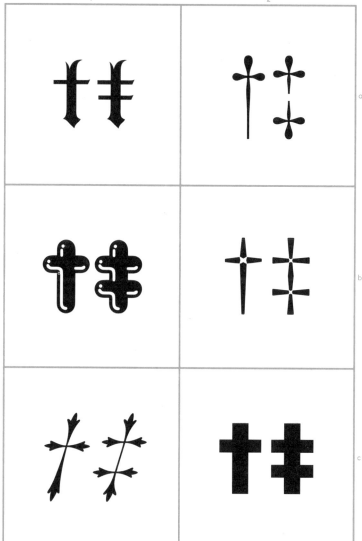

1a Agincourt Regular

1b Frankfurter Highlight

1c Bauer Bodoni Italic

2a Baskerville MT Pro Regular

2b Lirico Pro Semibold

2c Neue Haas Grotesk Dspl 95

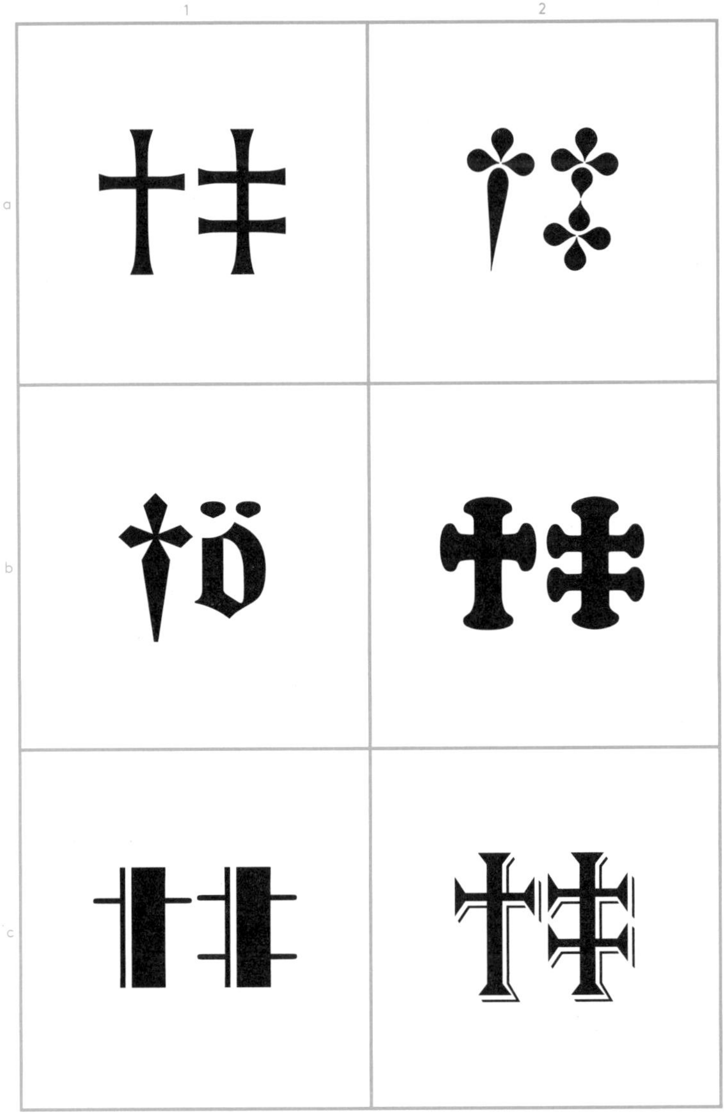

	1	2
a		
b		
c		

1a Albertus MT Pro Light
1b Wittenberger Fraktur Bold
1c Broadway Engraved BT
2a Balega Std
2b Cooper Black Roman
2c Algerian Condensed

a

b

c

3a Gill Sans Ultra Bold 3c A. Ali Regular 4b Kino MT Regular
3b Bodoni Std Poster 4a Amalia Pro Regular 4c Gill Sans Shadow Regular

Bullet — The history of the bullet point is unclear. Throughout the centuries, typographic flags, often in the form of points, separated unordered lists that did not require numbering. However, the term 'bullet' was not officially recognised until 1983, with the advent of early computer systems.

Bullet points are primarily used to add structure to a text by separating out different items in a list. In presentations and outlines, they are invaluable, as they can demarcate ideas or topics in a way that is immediately visually digestible. Bulleted items can be individual words, short phrases, full sentences or entire paragraphs. They do not have to have a full stop at the end unless they form complete sentences.

Prior to the use of word processors, asterisks or hyphens usually denoted bullets. Today, however, they can take on any number of forms: filled in circle, empty circle, diamond, square, tick, right arrow or right triangle, to name but a few.

1a Carrosserie Regular
1b Times New Roman Regular
1c Vectrex Big
2a GT Pressura Regular
2b Letterbox Pro
2c Magnifico Daytime ITC

¶

Pilcrow — The pilcrow, also known prosaically as the paragraph mark, indicates the start and finish of a paragraph. It is most commonly used in word processing programmes, as a non-permanent mark – i.e. a mark that does not show up in print. Despite its virtual invisibility, it has a lengthy history, reaching back to Ancient Greece, where the concept of a 'paragraph' pre-dated any other punctuation mark. The symbol itself is mostly likely derived from the Latin *capitula* (chapter), which was abbreviated to a large 'C'. To avoid confusion, the 'C' acquired a heavier curve, and a vertical bar through it, eventually evolving into the more elaborate sign we know today. The name 'pilcrow' is thought to have come from various corruptions of the word 'paragraph', or, more entertainingly, from the phrase 'pulled crow', due to its resemblance to a plucked bird.

The pilcrow was once used with great abandon, elaborately drawn in bright red ink by specialised rubricators. A manuscript would be left with wide blank spaces in which the rubricators would later draw the pilcrows. Eventually, paragraphs were started on new lines, with an indentation left for the pilcrow. When a rubricator ran out of time, the indentation was left blank, and eventually this became standard practice – the new line and the indentation taking the place of the fiddly pilcrow.

Today, the pilcrow's primary uses are in proofreading as an indication that a paragraph should be inserted, in legal texts, when citing a specific paragraph, and in academic writing, when citing from an HTML page.

§

Section sign — The section sign is a graphic ligature of two 'S's, an abbreviation of the Latin *signum sectionis*. It is generally used to refer to a specific section in a long document, and is most commonly used in the context of legal documentation. For example, §21 would refer the reader to Section 21. If Section 21 is lengthy, there might also be a pilcrow to refer the reader to a specific paragraph within the section (§21 ¶3). The section sign can also be duplicated to indicate a range of sections (§§ 21–27).

The section sign is also used in mathematical and computational contexts. Occasionally it will also be used as a marker for a footnote if the asterisk and dagger have already been used.

Hedera — The hedera, or fleuron, is an ancient glyph that was used in early Greek and Latin texts to signify a break between paragraphs, similar to the pilcrow. The hedera, which translates from Latin as 'ivy', looks like a floral heart with vine-like swirls around the top. It is very ornate, and to a large degree this was part of its appeal; as well as serving the purpose of marking paragraphs, it was also a cheap and effective way of breaking up text with ornamentation using a standardised printing block.

Today, although it is fairly uncommon, the hedera can be used to divide paragraphs, or as an ornamental way of breaking up lists. There are many different variants in hedera designs, and the mark can be placed vertically or horizontally as per preference.

1a ITC Zapf Dingbats Std   1c Goudy Sorts MT   2b Goudy Sorts MT
1b Goudy Sorts MT   2a Goudy Sorts MT   2c Arabesque Ornaments 1

Manicule — Derived from the Latin *maniculum*, or 'little hand', the manicule was used abundantly throughout the Renaissance and up until the 18th century. This pointing hand glyph drew readers' attention to important or interesting text, acting as an authorial guide through a document. The first known use of the manicule was in the *Domesday Book* of 1086, but it was only in the 14th century that it really took off. Humanist scholars embraced it enthusiastically, scrawling it in the margins of everything from law books to literature.

Although its basic form has remained intact through the centuries, there were countless interpretations of the mark, ranging from semi-abstract squiggly strokes to elaborate, stylised hands with ornate cuffs and flowing sleeves, in which a note about the note was sometimes written. With the advent of printing, the manicule gradually fell out of favour, giving way to the more pragmatic numbered footnote.

Today, the manicule is only rarely used. Now soberly decked in the cuff of a businessman, the manicule occasionally makes an appearance in signage and advertisements, in order to lend a vintage flavour, and also features on the return-to-sender stamps of the US Postal Service. One could argue that the little hand that acts as a cursor on some computers is a form of manicule, interfacing between the reader and the material on screen.

1a DF Calligraphic Ornaments   1c Type Embellishments Three   2b ITC Zapf Dingbats Std
1b DF Calligraphic Ornaments   2a Columbus Ornaments Two   2c ITC Zapf Dingbats Std

Plus-minus — The symbols for plus and minus are so common that it might come as a surprise that their introduction to our lexicon is relatively recent. The Ancient Greeks occasionally used the slash symbol for addition and a horizontal curve for subtraction, but by medieval times, these had been replaced with a simple 'P' and 'M'. The plus sign was introduced in the 15th century, derived from a simplification of the Latin et, meaning 'and'. The origin of the minus sign is less clear – it is thought that it might be derived from a tilde written over the letter 'M', or possibly a bar symbol used by merchants to separate the tare from the total weight of goods. Both are derived from Latin, meaning 'more' and 'less'.

Typographically, there have been many variations of the plus sign through the ages. Some have been more like a Latin cross and others have been quite ornate. The minus sign has always been simpler, although in many northern European countries, the obelus (÷) was used until fairly recently to indicate minus. The hyphen and the minus sign are often confused, but the minus sign is traditionally longer than the hyphen, generally designed at the same width as the plus sign in that font.

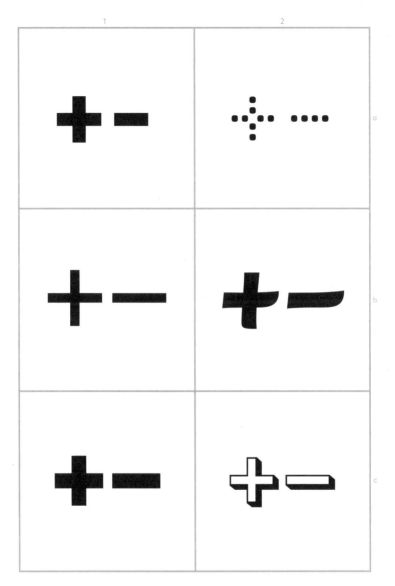

a

b

c

1a Buenos Aires Bold   1c Univers 93   2b Balega
1b Helvetica Neue W1G 67   2a A. ABF Petit Regular   2c Gill Sans Shadow Regular

÷

Obelus — The obelus is closely related to the dagger symbol (see pp. 48–51), and was used in ancient manuscripts to mark passages of dubious origin or to indicate deleted text. Its name is derived from the Greek for 'roasting spit'. As a continuation of its origins as a mark of omission, the obelus was used in Europe as the sign for subtraction, with some Scandinavian countries continuing to use it up until the 20th century.

In the 17th century, the German mathematician, Johann H Rahn, introduced it as a symbol of division in his book, *Teutsche Algebra*. With the publication of the English edition, the sign was appropriated in Britain and later America, becoming a standard representation of division in those countries. In many parts of the world, the obelus is not commonly used – the solidus or colon take on the role of division sign.

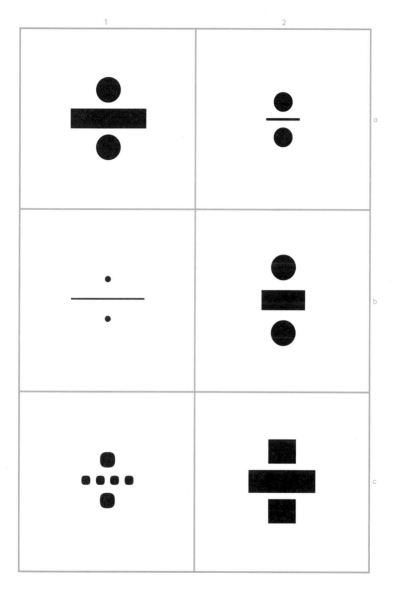

1a Banco Regular
1b SangBleu BP Hairline

1c A. ABF Petit Regular
2a Iwan Stencil Pro

2b Buenos Aires Bold
2c Neue Haas Grotesk Dspl 95

%

Percent — The percent sign indicates a fraction of 100, and its name is derived in origin from the Italian term *per cento*, meaning 'of a hundred'. In wealthy, 15th century Italy, 100 had become a common base for financial transactions, and scribes began to use the abbreviation 'pc' with the 'c' elongated and a little loop at its top end to represent the 'o' in *cento*. Over the next two centuries, the sign evolved into a combination of a loop and a horizontal bar. By the 19th century, the tilted fraction bar came into common usage.

In formal writing it is not generally acceptable to use the percent sign in running text – the word should be spelt out as percent, or per cent. The symbol should only be used in tables and in mathematical contexts, with occasional exceptions made for places with space restrictions. With regards to spacing, different rules apply in different languages. In English, there is no space between the number and the percent sign. Spanish and French, however, do require a space. In Persian and Turkish, the percent sign precedes the number.

a

b

c

1a Saphir Regular   1c Vectrex Medium   2b Broadway Engraved BT
1b Cadiz Medium   2a Libelle Pro Regular   2c Buenos Aires Bold

3a Bottleneck Regular   3c Stilla Regular   4b Glowworm Regular
3b American Typewriter Reg   4a Wittenberger Fraktur Bold   4c Cabarga Cursiva Regular

Infinity — The symbol for infinity is the lazy eight curve, also known as the lemniscate. This symbol has ancient roots, but was first used in a mathematical context in 1655 by English mathematician, John Wallis. It is thought that Wallis may have derived the symbol from the Roman numeral for 1,000, CIƆ, which was sometimes used to mean 'many'. Whether or not that is the case, there is little doubt that the interconnecting loops, wrapping endlessly around one another, visually illustrates the concept.

The symbol caught on, finding usage in various contexts, from tarot cards, to flags, to logos. In mathematics, it has come to represent potential infinity, rather than an actual infinite quantity.

1a Libelle Pro Regular   1c Cochin Bold   2b CaseStudyNo1 Pro Light
1b A. Ali Regular   2a Cadiz Medium   2c Gill Sans MT Pro Ultrabold

73

Degree — The degree symbol takes the form of a small, elevated 'o' and represents degrees of arc, temperature, latitude and longitude and alcohol proof. Its first documented use was in the 16th century, as part of a mathematical equation in which it was used as a zero exponent.

The spacing etiquette of the degree sign is as follows: In the case of degrees of arc, there is no intervening space (although a designer may wish to insert a thin space for the sake of clarity).

In the case of temperature, the setting varies, some insert a space between the number and the degree sign (10 °C), and others don't. However, when writing a temperature range, it is generally accepted that there is no spacing (15–20°C).

The degree sign should not be confused with a superscript 'o' or an ordinal indicator, which is used to denote ordinal numbers (first, second, third...). In many font faces they are identical, but in others they are distinct symbols.

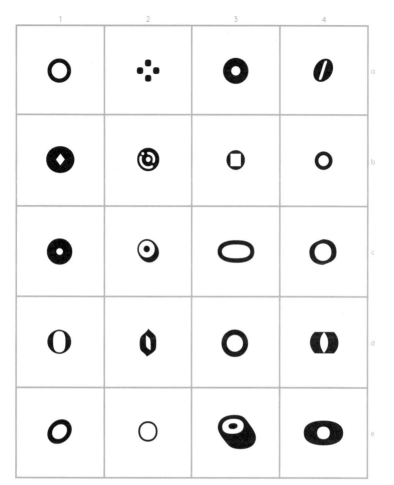

	1	2	3	4

1a Modern20 BT Roman
1b Beirut Poster
1c Glaser Stencil
1d Didot LF Roman
1e Univers 45 Light Oblique
2a A. ABF Petit Regular
2b Frankfurter Highlight

2c Cabaret Std Regular
2d Agincourt Regular
2e Neue Haas Grotesk Dspl 15
3a GT Walsheim Medium
3b CaseStudyNo1 Light
3c Braggadocio Regular
3d DIN 1451 Mittelschrift

3e Magnifico Daytime ITC
4a Stilla Regular
4b Albertus MT Pro Light
4c GT Sectra Fine Regular
4d Kino MT Regular
4e Antique Olive Nord

At sign — The graceful curl of the at sign is one of indeterminate origins. Some believe medieval monks used it as shorthand for the word *ad*, meaning 'toward' in Latin. Others say that it came from an abbreviation of 'each at', with the 'a' being encased in the 'e'. What is known for certain is that by the 16th century, @ was being used to denote 'amphora', a unit of liquid measurement named after Roman storage jars. By the 20th century, the symbol had become fairly obscure, used only occasionally by the mercantile classes to represent the word 'at' in a monetary context (2 apples @ 50p), until Ray Tomlinson, a young computer engineer, revived its fortunes. Working on an early incarnation of e-mail, Tomlinson sought a little-used symbol that would separate the addressee's name from the name of the computer. The visual clarity of the sign, coupled with its virtual obsolescence made it a prime candidate.

The @ sign is now a mainstay of modern communication. It is called the 'snail' in Italian and the 'monkey tail' in Dutch – indicators of its playful aesthetic. Logo designers embraced it with excessive gusto in the late '90s and early years of the 21st century, splashing it tackily on bad cafés and poorly thought through packaging, taking some of the shine off its curls. However, there is something appealing in the aesthetic of the first letter of the alphabet, embraced in a womb of its own making. It speaks of communication, intimacy and informality. Just like the medium it has come to represent.

a

b

c

d

1a Johnston ITC Std Bold
1b Lirico Pro Semibold
1c A. Ali Regular
1d Arcus Regular

2a Amalia Pro Regular
2b Fluo Regular
2c A. ABF Petit Regular
2d Mercury Bold

3a Agincourt Regular
3b Neue Haas Grotesk Dspl 95
3c A. Coupé Regular
3d Buenos Aires Bold

Underscore — The underscore is a relatively new symbol, which was introduced with the invention of the mechanical typewriter. In pre-computer days it was purely used to underline words or to create 'fill in the blank' lines. However, with the advent of character coding in the very early days of the computer, no white space was allowed, so the underscore, or 'break character' as it was then known, was used as a word separator. Today, the symbol continues to be used to create visual spacing when a white space is not permitted, for example, in the cases of e-mail addresses, Internet URLs and computer file names.

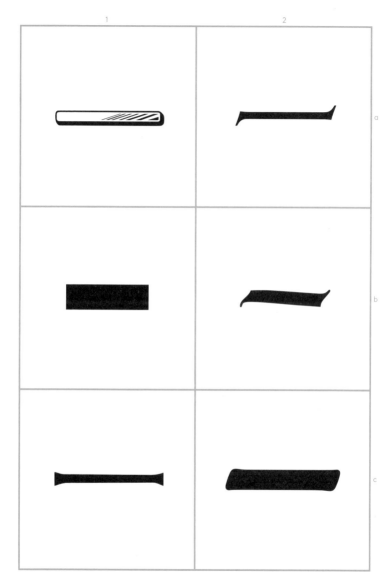

1a Cabaret Std Regular
1b Futura Extrabold

1c Albertus MT Pro Light
2a Cochin Pro Roman

2b Agincourt Regular
2c Cooper Black Roman

/

Prime — The prime symbol, which looks deceptively like a quotation mark, is used to represent units of feet, arcminutes and minutes. Its sibling, the double-prime symbol, represents smaller units of these measurements; inches, arcseconds and seconds.

The prime symbol should not be confused with the apostrophe, quotation mark, acute accent or grave. Nor should the double prime symbol be confused with the double quotation mark or the ditto mark. These are all individual typographic symbols.

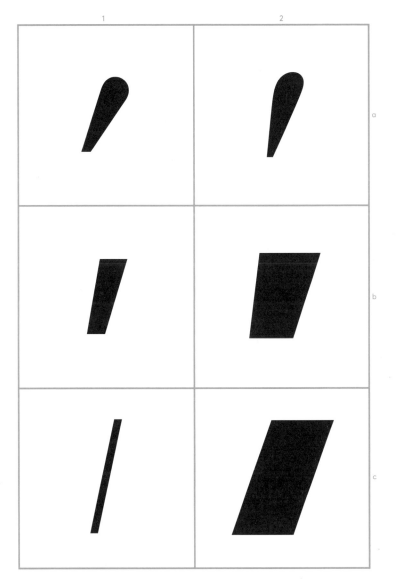

1a Palatino Linotype Bold   1c Neue Haas Grotesk Dspl 15   2b Neue Haas Unica ExtraBlack
1b Neue Haas Unica Regular   2a Palatino Linotype Regular   2c Neue Haas Grotesk Dspl 96

81

#

The hashtag, octothorpe or pound sign, comes from the Latin abbreviation lb, short for *libra pondo*, or 'pound weight'. It was first used around the 14th century and was written with a short stroke above the letters so that the 'l' would not be mistaken for a '1'. This gradually morphed into # – the bottom line implying the bottom of the 'l and b' and the top line referring to the stroke above.

The symbol was integrated into technology in the late '60s by Bell Labs, inventors of the touch-tone phone, who used it in phone systems to separate between strings of numbers. Legend has it that the director of Bell Labs came up with the name 'octothorpe' by combining the figure's eight points with the surname of his favourite athlete, Olympian Jim Thorpe.

The hash then appeared in the early days of the internet, featuring as early as 1988, in networks where users communicated through channels, the subject of which was indicated by the hash sign (#Tokyo was a channel of people talking about Tokyo). By the new millennium, however, hashtags were not widely used online except by the techno-elite. In 2007, an employee at Twitter suggested prefixing the names of groups or 'channels' with a #. This suggestion was initially rejected as alienating and over-techie, but was eventually adopted, and the meteoric rise of the hashtag was set in motion.

a

b

c

1a A. Coupé Regular   1c Glowworm Regular   2b Letterbox Pro
1b Stoneheure Regular   2a Magnifico Daytime ITC   2c Balega Regular

Λ

Caret — Derived from the Latin *caret*, meaning 'it lacks', the caret symbol indicates where a word, phrase or punctuation mark is missing from a document. It has been used through the ages as a proofreading mark, and is traditionally inserted under the place where material is missing, with the absent material written above the line of text or in the margin. Where a high-level punctuation mark, such as an apostrophe, is missing, an inverted caret is used above the text. In mathematics, the caret represents an exponent, square, cube or other power. In text relating to computer usage, a caret represents the control key (^S = CTRL S).

A variant of the caret is the circumflex, which is used to indicate tonal accents in many languages including French, Welsh, Portuguese and Romanian. The circumflex is placed on top of the accented letter, and is also known as a 'hat'.

1a Glowworm Regular
1a Broadway BT Regular

1c Glaser Stencil
2a Stoneheure Regular

2a Libelle Pro Regular
2c Stilla Regular

~

Tilde — The term tilde, known informally as the squiggly, is derived from the Latin *titulus*, meaning 'title'. It was used in medieval times to indicate abbreviation. Due to the time-consuming nature of handwritten text, and the resulting proliferation of abbreviations, tildes were used extensively. When an 'n' or an 'm' followed a vowel, that letter was omitted, and a tilde was placed over the vowel (hence its resemblance to a little 'n'). It was also used over a 'q' as an abbreviation of the word *que* (meaning 'that').

Today, the symbol is used in various contexts in a minor capacity. It is occasionally used to indicate approximation; 7~10 strawberries means anywhere between seven strawberries and ten, inclusively. ~31 means approximately 31. Economists use the tilde to indicate that there is no preference between two products. X ~ Y means that both the products are rated of equivalent desirability. Its most common use is as a diacritical mark in Spanish, where it is used over the 'n' to create an 'nye' sound. It is also used as a diacritical mark in Portuguese and Estonian. In addition to this, the tilde is used in a wide range of IT-related applications.

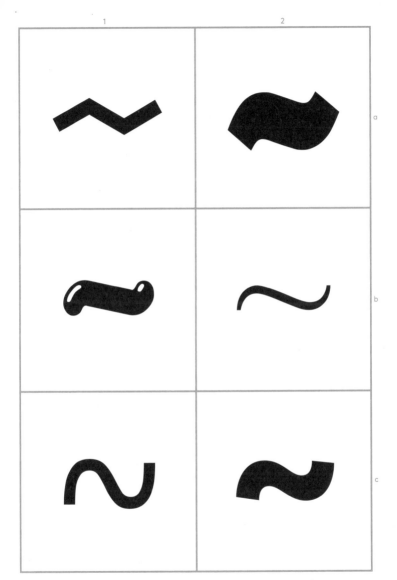

1a A. Ali Regular   1c ITC Symbol Book SC   2b Bell MT Regular
1b Glowworm Regular   2a Britannic Ultra Regular   2c Cadiz Bold

№

Numero sign — **Numero is a single Unicode character comprised of a capital 'N' and a small superscript 'o'. It is an abbreviation of the word** *numero*, **which is Latin for number, and, in the context of a spoken sentence, is read as 'number'. The symbol is used in ordinal numerations in most** European languages. In America the role of the numero sign is primarily fulfilled by the hashtag.

The presentation of the numero sign varies from font to font. Some place a small line under the 'o', to avoid confusion with the word 'no'. Others just use the superscript.

1a Buenos Aires Bold   1c Livorno Poster   2b GT Walsheim Medium
1b Custodia Pro Normal   2a Times New Roman Italic   2c Cochin Regular

91

©

Copyright — The copyright symbol indicates that exclusive rights are granted to the author or creator of a work. It was first widely used with the introduction of the copyright act of 1909. This act stated that the word 'copyright' had to physically appear on any work, in order to legally protect it from infringement. Artist organisations were understandably horrified at the prospect of defacing their masterpieces with the word 'copyright', and so a compromise was reached by allowing a discreet 'c' within a circle to appear next to the artist's name. This was initially only valid on artworks, but by the 1950s permission of use was extended to all other mediums.

Today, it is not necessary to display a copyright notice, as the creation of any work automatically establishes copyright. However, a copyright symbol is often used in order to inform the public that a work is protected by copyright. This way, if a work is infringed, there can be no defence based on innocent infringement.

The copyright symbol is formed of the letter 'c' inside a circle, signifying the protection the symbol offers to the owner of the work. It is generally followed by the year the work was created and the name of the creator. Copyright for sound recordings is indicated with a 'p' inside a circle (for phonorecord).

	1	2	3
a	©	©	©
b	©	©	©
c	©	▣	©
d	©	©	©

1a Helvetica Neue W1G 55
1b Futura Black
1c Glaser Stencil
1d Britannic Bold

2a Stoneheure Regular
2b Buenos Aires Bold
2c Screenex Regular
2d Balega Std

3a Modern20 BT Roman
3b Libelle Pro Regular
3c Cooper Black Roman
3d Agincourt Regular

TM

Trademark — **The trademark symbol is used to alert to the public that the preceding logo or mark belongs to you. Unlike the ®, which is reserved for marks registered in the Patent and Trademark Office, the ™ sign is used for unregistered trademarks. This means that effectively anyone can use the ™ sign, and it does not guarantee that the owner's mark will be protected under trademark laws.**

The trademark sign is generally placed in superscript next to the top right hand corner of a logo, occasionally migrating to the bottom right hand corner. It can look quite messy, especially when a logo features in a small format. However, many companies feel that beyond the assertion of copyright, it also suggests a heavier, more powerful corporate identity. Ultimately it is a matter of personal preference.

1a Bottleneck Regular   1c Helvetica Neue W1G 55   2b Larish Neue Semibold
1b Agincourt Regular   2a A. ABF Petit Regular   2c Balega Regular

Type Foundries Index

Broadway BT
BroadwayEngraved BT
Cabaret Std
Cabarga Cursiva
CaseStudiNo1 Pro
Caslon 224 Std ITC
Century Regular
Cochin
Colonna MT
Columbus Ornaments Two
Cooper Black
Didot Pro
Din 1451
Diotima
DF Calligraphic Ornaments
Folio Md BT
Founder's Caslon 42 ITC
Frankfurter Highlight
Futura CE Condensed
Futura
Gill Sans Ultra
Gill Sans MT Pro
Glaser Stencil
Glowworm
Goudy Old Style MT
Helvetica Neue
Imprint MT Shadow
Iwan Stencil Pro
Johnston ITC Pro
Libelle Pro
Kino MT
Lydian BT
Magnifico Daytime ITC Std
Modern 20 BT
Monotype Corsiva
Neue Haas Grotesk
Neue Haas Unica
News Gothic MT
OCR A
Palatino Linotype
Plantin Infant MT
Runic MT
Saphir
Stilla

Symbol Book SC ITC
Times New Roman
Type Embellishments 3
Univers
Wittenberger Fraktur
Zapf Dingbats Std ITC

NOUVELLE NOIRE
nouvellenoire.ch

A. ABF Petit
A. Ali
A.Coupé

OUR TYPE
ourtype.com

Amalia Pro
Arnhem Pro
Custodia Pro
Lirico Pro

RADIM PEŠKO
radimpesko.com

Larish Neue
Mercury

SWISS TYPEFACES
swisstypefaces.com

NewParis KingSize
NewParis Text
SangBleu BP

Acknowledgements